Yosemite

of The Promise Wildness

Yosemite

The Promise
of
Wildness

PHOTOGRAPHS BY William Neill
ESSAY BY Tim Palmer

YOSEMITE
ASSOCIATION

Yosemite National Park, California

Library of Congress Cataloging-in-Publication Data
Neill, William.
Yosemite: the promise of wildness/
photographs by William Neill: essay by Tim Palmer.
p. cm.
ISBN 0-939666-77-4
1. YosemiteNational Park (Calif.)—Pictorial works.
2. Yosemite National Park (Calif.)
I. Palmer, Tim   II. Title
F868.Y6N45   1994

917.94'47'00222–dc20   94–21789
                         CIP

10 9 8 7 6 5 4 3 2 1

Design by TENAZAS DESIGN, San Francisco.
Printed in Hong Kong.

LIMITED EDITION PHOTOGRAPHS
Limited edition photographic prints of William Neill
images reproduced in this book are available from the artist.
For orders or inquiries, contact the artist in care
of the Yosemite Association.

Yosemite Association
P.O. Box 545
Yosemite National Park, CA 95389

The Yosemite Association is a non-profit, membership
organization dedicated to the support of Yosemite National
Park. Our publishing program is designed to provide an
educational service and to increase the public's understanding
of Yosemite's special qualities and needs. To learn more
about our activities and other publications, or for information about membership, please write to the address above,
or call (209) 379-2646.

To Ansel, for his vision and commitment;

   to the spirit of Yosemite and those who cherish and strive to preserve it;

and to Sadhna.

W. N.

Contents

Only
One
Yosemite

Yosemite, once again, lies waiting to be discovered. The rivers rush down from the peaks, the pines whistle in the breeze, the cliffsides gleam in sunset's golden light. Though it seems that just about everybody has discovered Yosemite, the pleasure can take fresh form with every visit; it can lead to a new kind of awareness. The more you look, the more you find, and it is important that every soul can find pleasure and joy in this heartwarming, joyous place.

Equally important are the new discoveries that lie waiting in regard to our care for Yosemite. More than a hundred years after establishment of this national park for the preservation of its scenery, it is again timely to realize the importance of the view spread out before us, of its value to our civilization, and of new possibilities for protection of this once-in-a-world place.

Awaiting a New Discovery

The promise of preservation, made long ago and reaffirmed through the ages, is one that must be rediscovered with each new era in our relationship with this land. The promise of wildness is one that can still be met. Unfortunately, the passing years bring more difficult problems as the human pressures increase here in the "Range of Light," as pioneering preservationist John Muir called the Sierra Nevada.

Reverence for an Extraordinary Place

In all its wonder and contradictions, this enrapturing geography lies mountainbound as the quintessential scenery, the first significant landscape protected by law in America, and a sanctuary for today's believers in the natural world. Here is the heart of the Sierra Nevada—at the mid-point of the range's 400-mile-long expanse of unbroken high country from Lake Almanor in the north to the Tehachapi Mountains in the south. Yosemite ranks among the most-visited national parks and is a hotbed of concern to people who take our stewardship of the Earth seriously. Emblematic of both the unspoiled Eden and the incessant demands placed upon it by an expanding and growth-obsessed society, Yosemite stands preeminently as a symbol of nature amid civilization.

The symbol is one of unencumbered mountains, exquisite valleys, wild canyons, resin-scented forests, glassy rivers, thunderous waterfalls with chilling mist, towering rock walls, and yellow-green meadows lying in embraceable softness, all of it home to a wealth of native plants and wildlife—in total, an ecosystem of stunning complexity and beauty. It is a special place. And because of this, Yosemite has been the subject of popular wisdom, evocative prose, great American art, public policy, and congressional action. John Muir—the father of the land preservation movement in America—called Yosemite "the most striking and sublime" scene in the Sierra. He referred to Yosemite Valley as the "grandest of all the special temples of nature." He repeatedly described the Valley and the nearby sequoia groves as "cathedrals," as did many other writers.

Even in the first documented account of Yosemite, in 1851, Lafayette Bunnell wrote, "I have here seen the power and glory of a supreme being ... This seemed God's holiest temple." More recent visitors, encountering not only the temple but also the trappings of a destination resort complete with the hassle and clutter that they thought they had left back home, have been less inclined toward the prose of the sacred. Yet, of the modern era, California historian Kevin Starr commented, "Yosemite still engenders in the majority of Americans a feeling of reverence and awe."

The park's chief naturalist for twenty years, Leonard McKenzie observed, "Yosemite evokes a sense of inspiration, wonder, and mystique. Some call it magical." With a perceptive understanding of both the place and its effect on people, he added, "Among the Earth's distinctive places, this showcase occupies a special niche in the human spirit ... "

Having similar professional and personal ties to the park, Donald Fox, Yosemite's long-time landscape architect, wrote of the unusual power conveyed by the place. "Yosemite Valley is a symbol. It engraves powerful images upon our minds and evokes feelings of love, care and respect. Yosemite is also a sacred place, a place for pilgrimage, for renewing the human spirit, for enriching human life."

This valley of meadow vistas, idyllic forests, and peaceful riverfront has no equal, with its surroundings of cliffs, waterfalls, and high country. Here the combination of prospect owing to open views, and refuge owing to sheltering groves and canyon enclaves, is found in perfection.

Landscapes of America's other great mountain ranges—the Rockies, Cascades, Coastal Ranges, Appalachians, Alaska Range, and Brooks Range—lack the remarkable mixture of eye-dazzling components of Yosemite's rich scenery. Since Hetch Hetchy Valley was flooded by a reservoir in the northern reaches of the park, no similar sites exist even in the Sierra Nevada. Yosemite is cherished, probably more than any other valley in America, as a paragon of scenery, a landscape for reverence, and a holy place.

In this book, photographs by William Neill transport the intrigue of Yosemite into people's homes everywhere, perhaps as effectively as pages of paper can. From sweeping vistas to intimate studies of natural phenomena, his images strongly convey Yosemite's exceptional qualities. They also illustrate the wealth of the ecosystem that, through the interrelationship of plant, animal and landscape, forms an artful mosaic. Scenes of detail indicate the beauty that is found in all undeveloped corners of the park. Some views typify Yosemite alone, while others emblematize natural wonders that searchers can discover in unspoiled environments everywhere. The latter impart one of the greatest lessons of Yosemite: not just this place, but the whole Earth is worth appreciating. Perhaps these images will convince viewers that the preservation of Yosemite for the singular values it offers to our society should be the foremost goal in our relationship with this astonishing but small piece of Earth.

Exploring the Boundaries of Beauty

If Yosemite holds importance in our society today, it's because the place is so different. While beautiful landscapes exist everywhere they are not ruined by abuse, Yosemite is so perfectly beautiful. It meets so many expectations of dreamland, of a fantasy world. What makes these 1,169 square miles of protected real estate so different? What set of values do they offer to our society? What lessons can be learned by opening our lives and minds to all that this place has to offer? At all times of year and in all parts of the park, I've sought to answer the questions.

IN SEPTEMBER, after the frosty breath of autumn had begun to settle across the high country, I set out for the summit of Mount Conness in the northern realms of Yosemite. Rising cloud-like from the Sierra crest, the mountain's elegant eastern spine drew me upward, past lakes and over slabs of granite, onto scree slopes and then to a bony spine of rock bridging two sections of the summit. Finally I scrambled to the top.

I looked downward with amazement and controlled fear. Streams stretched to the southwest as though scratched out by giant claws pulled toward the Tuolumne River. Marked by folds in the mountains, the river continued in a granite-domed, canyon-clad course down the Sierra's western slope. The east side of the Sierra—one of the most dramatic fault blocks on the continent—dropped as in a free-fall from the escarpment to the basin of the celebrated Mono Lake.

Though biologically esteemed, the lake has been depleted to supply water to Los Angeles, 338 miles away. To the south, the grandeur of Yosemite National Park stretched out as if in layers of mountain scenery, one behind the other in progressively lighter shades, a paradise within protective political boundaries. From Conness, however, the boundaries made no sense. It was geography and ecosystems I saw.

The lesson of this climb was less one of mountaineering than it was of awareness that the park is a whole piece, so sinuously interconnected, and that the connections—vital to all resident life—extend beyond politically-created lines. When we protect a park, should we protect the life of that park, the context of that park? Should we protect its ecosystem? I would seek the answers to these and other questions in seasons to come as I grew to know Yosemite better.

———————

FOR MY SECOND VIEW of the park, I returned when the willows shone yellow and brilliant in October's sun, when a skim of ice encircled mountain lakes and ponds. I caught a ride with other travelers to Tuolumne Meadows, beneath peaks that rose above the deepest ice masses of the glaciers, thus avoiding the rounded polish given to other summits nearby. Above the meadows, near the highest road-accessible pass in the Sierra, I set out on foot for the high divide between the Tuolumne and Merced rivers. At dusk, I made camp at the edge of a meadow, and beneath the stars, I began to sleep, expecting nothing but the slumbering peace of the mountains.

The thud of my food bag hitting the ground awoke me with a start. A black bear had swatted it from its perch in a tree and knocked it down. Clutching the bag with formidable teeth, my shadowy visitor ran away. I pursued for a while, then thought differently about the plan when I entered a garden of bear-sized boulders that all assumed animate form, like a dozen bears awaiting me in the dim light of a quarter-moon. I became acutely aware that I shared this place with

The more you look, the more

other creatures—some of them large. More accurately, the bear shared its home with me. Familiarity with human food on the part of animals—unhealthy for wildlife and distressing to campers—has been one unfortunate result of this sharing of territory. Nonetheless, I could not suppress a smile in the knowledge that the Sierra stood as mountains of life, to which I was merely a vulnerable visitor.

In the morning, my courage fed by daylight and the force of necessity, I recovered my provisions, most of them uneaten (the bear presumably dissatisfied with my unadorned lentils, rice, and oats). I scooped up my food and continued on my way.

My way led to three days of paradisiac rambling among the high lakes and craggy ridges of the upper Merced. My pattern would surely have appeared aimless to anyone watching from afar, and it was. One of the beauties, here, is that no one was around to notice. When the time came to go, I wended my way down the river-flume of whitewater, past swimming holes that seemed to suck me to the center of the earth, and beneath rainbow-gated waterfalls, all of it ending in Yosemite Valley, frosty in the mornings as beds of ferns turned their autumn color in fields of gold.

———————

IN NOVEMBER, after high country travel became risky owing to early season snowstorms, I drove to the northwestern reaches of the park. Here, in what had been the twin of Yosemite Valley in John Muir's day, contractors for the City of San Francisco had erected O'Shaughnessy Dam, which formed Hetch Hetchy Reservoir. The project had been the focus of the opening battle for the protection of parklands, wilderness, and rivers in America. John Muir had led the unsuccessful campaign to prevent the dam from flooding the Hetch Hetchy Valley. Now, flatwater covers his haunts of meadow and forest. Tributaries still pour their waterfalls from canyon rims, but the effect is one of pathetic contrast as lapping water erodes the shore of the reservoir, burying the beauty of Yosemite Valley's closest scenic counterpart.

An unsung loss in this dim chapter of national park history was Eleanor Creek. Northwest of Hetch Hetchy, this granite-sculpted stream was interred beneath a second reservoir that raised the level of a natural lake. A third dam, just outside Yosemite on Cherry Creek, eliminated a migration route for deer herds of the park.

San Francisco officials had argued that flooding Hetch Hetchy Valley would serve the interests of the greatest number of people. Their reasoning and political muscle persuaded Department of Interior officials and Congress, in spite of substantial nationwide opinion that the natural qualities of Yosemite National Park warranted preservation.

Perhaps the greatest tragedy, and the greatest lesson for the future, was that alternative sources for water supply were available elsewhere. Our society sacrificed a place of rare quality for

you find, and it is important that every heart can

development that could have adequately been provided at less extraordinary sites. While national parks are no longer endangered by new dams, the lesson applies to other threats today.

———————

IN LATE FEBRUARY, at the southern end of the park, the trail to Ostrander Lake Hut lay beneath five feet of snow, and the white smoothness led me outward to free-form winter wanderings in the backcountry. The snow hid rocks, logs, and brush, enabling a skier to range almost anywhere short of avalanche slopes. One moves randomly and unfettered through a space, rather than on a line. The lines of roads, trails, and boardwalks elsewhere constrain us and have us looking more at the ground than around us, more concerned with following someone else's path than with discovering our own.

Skiing south and east for three days, I was pulled onward by scenes of the Clark Range, until high on its corniced ridges, my view encompassed the peaks and forests of the park, cut by the canyons of the South Fork of the Merced and other tributaries leading to sequoia groves in lower country. Down there, the Merced River burst forcefully from its snowy source in the Yosemite backcountry and flowed ribbon-like in white foam, emerald depths, and graniteboulder-stops. In that valley, springtime would soon begin with snowmelt and the first shoots of green.

IN LATE MARCH, a balmy week of sunshine seemed to have announced winter's end. Rock climbers from around the world gravitate to Yosemite for the challenge of its monolithic granite walls, and now, tempted by the radiant warmth, a trio of climbers set out to scale the south face of Half Dome—a 2,000 foot exposed cliff on the back side of the rock's famous visage.

The blue skies yielded to clouds, to rain, to freezing rain, and then to snow, and snow, and snow. Despite efforts to contend with the bad weather, the climbers became ice-bound in slings hanging from frozen ropes, then lost their ability to save themselves.

As part of a rescue team, I departed Yosemite Valley at 11 p.m., my pack consisting of a bulky bundle of ten pairs of snowshoes. With head lamps modestly beaming the way, our team of ten people slogged in fresh snow and splashed through swollen creeks halfway up to our knees, the water repelled by gaiters worn over our boots. Another team forged the way ahead of us, and a third team came behind. My hiking partner, Tim Ludington, worked as a trail crew foreman on his day-

find pleasure and joy in this heartwarming, joyous place.

time shift and knew the trail well. He pointed out a black void to our immediate left, and shouted above the roar of water. "That's a thousand-foot drop-off."

At 2 a.m., for a change of pace, some of us traded packs. I relinquished my ungainly load, but received fifty pounds of rope—half of a 1,600-foot-long line that would presumably be used, by someone other than me, to drop by rappel from the top of Half Dome and down to the ledge where the climbers waited. The other half of the rope was carried by a stranger named Willy, with whom I was now connected on this dark, stormy night by a short coil of slack line that I held in my hand. In a short time we got to know each other well.

Just before dawn, we surfaced from a snow-enshrouded forest and stepped onto the open face of the "pre-dome," beneath the rise of Half Dome itself. This inhospitable spot was terrifically frightening and terrifically beautiful.

On snowshoes now, we shuffled upward to a flat bench while the earliest light broke yellow and blue on the weightless flakes of perfect crystals that everywhere softened that rocky universe.

As it turned out, our hard-earned presence was superfluous. We cheered while a helicopter crew rescued the cold climbers. As I watched, I reflected on Yosemite, not only as a place of ecosystems and beauty, but as one of opportunity, cooperation, and humbleness in nature's arms. Even though these were abstract ideas, all seemed to require a place in order to exist.

THE SPLENDOR OF SPRINGTIME was reflected in hot April afternoons and in balmy evenings cooled by the chill downdraft of mountain air. At that turning point of dusk, I arrived at the Mariposa Grove of Giant Sequoias, on the southern boundary of the park.

The enormous girth and height of the trees were accentuated when the sequoias turned to black etchings against a navy blue, twilight sky. Lacking meaningful perspective in that forest full of mammoth trees, I walked up to one, spread my arms against its furrowed bark, and felt only the slightest turn of a curve in the trunk. It is difficult to hug a sequoia tree—the largest organism on earth.

Even more impressive than individual bulk or size, however, was the aggregate forest of sequoia trees. Singly, in pairs, and in groups, they sheltered that mountainside as only the giants of the world can do. Between them grew sugar pines—skyscrapers in their own right, some reaching 250 feet tall, the largest of all pines.

Shrouded by growing darkness, I strolled deeper into the forest, and deeper, the silhouettes now subtle against a starlit sky. The springtime scent of wet soil stirred childhood memories of plowed fields. The nostalgic odor seemed to announce how vital the fertile forest is to a variety of life—not just to the spotted owl, gray squirrel, and fisher that frequent the branches of the shadowy kingdom, but also, for example, to millions of microbes within the dirt surrounding the sequoia root system, microbes on which the whole sequoia depends. The giant trees that drew me into that woodland had come to symbolize all forests and all the interconnected webs of life that forests house.

IN THE WELCOME HEAT OF EARLY JUNE, spring had burst from wildflower gardens valley-wide, and the Merced River ran thunderously in a symphony of snowmelt. Without the snow, the rain, and the runoff, Yosemite would be a desert, more like Zion National Park in Utah. The Sierra would be uncarved by glaciers and uncut by canyons, more like the White and Inyo Mountains just to the east. With the rich runoff raked from clouds bearing Pacific moisture, the park had life and music and an abundance of liquid sights that prompted me to stare, mesmerized, not just at waterfalls, but at rapids, pools, eddies, wetlands, puddles, dripping branches, soggy sedges, misted ferns, and dew-coated grass.

Tumbling down from the high country, the waters accumulate nutrients and microscopic beings that feed larger forms of life. The Tuolumne River, for example, becomes one of the finest trout fisheries in California. And beyond their immediate shores, the rivers support riparian thickets of willows, cottonwoods, and wetland greenery, so picturesque in Yosemite Valley, so essential to the larger ecosystem. The rivers are the arteries.

I ventured farther up the Merced, and with its bountiful springtime volume, the river plunged over Vernal Fall, mist raining across the canyon and drenching me, a rainbow of vivid color arching across the gulf in space carved by the river as it rushed downward toward Yosemite Valley.

Yosemite National Park may be the scenic highlight of America, and Yosemite Valley is the highlight of the Park. The Valley is the elegant climax to the entire Sierra, and, for that matter, to anything. Cliffs rise skyward. Waterfalls leap over the rim to be pushed aside by winds and then

Eden's Two Faces

to smash onto rocks and hiss outward as riffling rivers, bubbling, glistening, perfectly clear. Ponderosa pines put on the weight of cambium easily and achieve a statuesque thickness in shady groves at meadow edges. And the meadows—they stretch up and down. From their centers the world of cliffs, waterfalls, and forests seems to revolve as in the kaleidoscope of childhood dreams, pure landscape fantasy, the kinds of dreams one might choose to die with given adequate presence of mind. Put simply,

Yosemite Valley is for many people a vision of Eden, of heaven, of paradise.

This is Yosemite Valley as it once was and as it remains in sites of isolation. In my visits to the Valley, I always seek out special epicenters of scenery: the utterly sacred Leidig Meadow, the precipitous cliffs above Yosemite Falls, the wind-blessed base of Bridalveil Fall, the open elegance of El Capitan Meadow, the tranquil Merced at Cathedral Rocks. But the Valley is much more than these carefully selected views. This time, I want to see the whole thing.

Striving to overlook nothing, I spend a day walking through the place from end to end. At the Valley's uppermost reach, the Happy Isles Nature Center is a building reached only by shuttle bus, uncompromised by other traffic. My path soon enters Upper Pines, the first of five campgrounds that run back-to-back for about three miles of meandering Merced River frontage. Near this camping city with one, two, and sometimes three cars per site, is Curry Village, a complex of 628 overnight units and related facilities stretching for half a mile beneath the splendid granite apron of Glacier Point.

Nearby, Stoneman Meadow beckons as a grassy enclave, a quarter-mile long. Just downriver from the campgrounds is Housekeeping Camp—280 overnight units that consist of tent fabric attached to concrete walls. The lower row of these semi-permanent tents almost reaches the Merced River's bank, which has been rip-rapped with rocks like those streams declared nuisances in urban areas. In deference to the tent-cabins, boulders have been dumped here to prevent the Merced's natural claim to its flood plain.

The Ahwahnee Hotel lies across the river and to the north, a stately 99-room luxury facility with 24 cottage units sprinkled in the nearby woods of fir and pine. Guests at the hotel enjoy views of spectacular cliffs just outside the windows. To the southwest lies the Camp 6 complex of tents, house trailers, chain-link fences, a construction-material-boneyard, and parked semi-truck trailers, from which the view to Half Dome is spectacular.

Yosemite is also a sacred place,
a place for pilgrimage,
for renewing the
human spirit,
for enriching human life.

Ahwahnee Meadow runs for a quarter-mile, bordered by frame houses and an apartment complex for the concessionaire's full-time staff. This neighborhood is adjoined by a bus garage and fire department, and then by a grocery and general store, gift shop, hamburger stand, deli, pizza and ice cream store, post office, Park Service visitor center, Park Service office buildings, warehouses, heavy equipment parking areas, school, and ranger housing—the total agglomeration of Yosemite Village and related infrastructure continuing for nearly a mile. Much of this can be avoided by adhering to the riverfront or to strips of meadows, though roads flank the river and

the meadows on either side, and the loudspeaker of an open-air tram regularly announces scenery that I prefer to identify on my own or leave unnamed.

Past Yosemite Village, I cross Yosemite Creek, and just beyond I walk through the Yosemite Lodge complex. Here, 495 overnight units can be found in motels and cabins, along with employee housing, a swimming pool, and other amenities. This half-mile-long improved site culminates in a 15-pump gas station.

The lower four miles of the Valley are mostly undeveloped and include the splendor of Leidig Meadow with its views to Yosemite Falls, Half Dome, and Sentinel Rock. Farther down the Valley lie the granite monolith of El Capitan and the framed beauty of Bridalveil Fall. Two roads, however, run the length of the Valley, which is only half a mile wide. The greatest distance a person may escape from a paved roadway is 1,000 feet—less than one-fifth of a mile, or the length of a city block. A one-way road enters the Valley on the south side, the other road exits the Valley on the north side. The paralleling roads each carry heavy loads of cars and busses in a constant stream of traffic. Thus, any walk across Yosemite Valley requires two busy road crossings. It is dangerous to claim superlatives for any landscape, but it seems safe to say that Yosemite Valley is, indeed, the most beautiful median strip in the world.

There are two ways of looking at all this. The first is to appreciate that the scenery captures the eye as some of the most breathtaking in the world. One's view can overtop the roads and the buildings and see the cliffs and the falls. One can walk off the roads and the bike paths and onto trails that cross the meadows.

The second approach is to observe that almost any view in the Valley includes at least some evidence of roads or buildings or both. Through the middle third of the Valley—the section most blessed with scenic wonders—it is only by gazing at details on the ground or by telescoping our vision outward to sublime landmarks that we are afforded a view lacking the cars, pavement, and buildings that typify the cities that people have abandoned. To enjoy the natural scene only, we must crop off the foreground, or the left, or the right—and usually all three—as we create our contrived frame of reference.

For a more satisfying view of the Valley, I sought out one of the spots most distant from roads or development. On Sunday afternoon, while latecomers still entered and other visitors began their return to California cities, the sounds of traffic were loud on both sides of the Valley. But I

The Question of Intrinsic Values

focused on the scene, on the abridged version of beauty before me.

The river riffled past, as peaceful as in the paradise of my mind's eye. The Merced's sibilance marked an interlude between its crashing drops from the Sierra high country and its tumultuous rush down the gorge below. A ponderosa pine grew rigidly out of the fertile soil to shelter me as I leaned against its great, golden-barked trunk and stared at the soaring rise of El Capitan, white and gleaming, regarded as the largest exposed mass of granite in the world. I felt incredibly good inside, both shielded and excited by what lay around me.

Here, I may be convinced that Yosemite has been preserved and managed for its highest intrinsic values—for the effect that its natural features have on the human spirit. But I was puzzled by the question: Is Yosemite Valley regarded as a revered place, or is it simply used as a better backdrop for recreation and tourism? Is this a place of pilgrimage, or just a backdrop of cliffs and waterfalls, a scenic resort like those we find at Tahoe, Mammoth, or Monterey?

While many people no longer come to Yosemite because of the crowds and development, the Valley remains a place of reverence even to them. All the while, the numbers of visitors grow and the management of the park is adjusted to serve them.

Now that I had seen Yosemite in all its seasons, from its remote landforms and from its most popular asphalt strips, I stopped to wonder. Can this Valley accommodate the crowds of the future and still survive as a sacred and special place?

Portfolio
One

Clearing summer storm clouds

Gates of the Valley

Black oaks in autumn

El Capitan Meadow

Cottonwoods

Yosemite Falls

Half Dome at sunset

From Olmsted Point

Confluence of Tamarack
and Cascade Creeks

Above the Merced River

Cathedral Rocks from the base of El Capitan

Yosemite Valley

Redbud

**Merced River
Canyon**

Black oaks and granite wall

Yosemite Valley

Black oak leaves

El Capitan Meadow

Sequoia trees and dogwood

**Tuolumne Grove of
Giant Sequoias**

Juniper and lichen-covered boulder

**Grand Canyon of the
Tuolumne River**

Half Dome and pine in clouds
Washburn Point

Morning clouds

Yosemite Valley

Winter sunset reflections in the Merced River

Gates of the Valley

Winter sunset, El Capitan and Merced River

Gates of the Valley

Clearing winter storm

Sentinel Rock

Yellow pines in snow

Yosemite Valley

Floating ice and cliffs

**Ellery Lake, Inyo
National Forest**

Glacial erratic and clouds
Near Tenaya Lake

Glacial erratics, late afternoon light
Near Olmsted Point

Cedars
and rock circle

Merced River

Cloud reflections and grasses
Tuolumne Meadows

Maple tree

Vernal Fall

Dogwood tree blooming
along the Merced River

Yosemite Valley

Clouds and reflections

Cathedral Rocks

The
Promise
of
Preservation

In 1864, Abraham Lincoln signed the legislation establishing the Yosemite Grant for the "preservation both of the Yosemite Valley and the Big Tree Grove." At that early date, the promise of preservation had been made.

Surrounded by the horrors of the Civil War, the President's action can be regarded as a recognition that no matter how difficult our straits as a society, we can turn to our native landscape for peace, for beauty, and for hope. Though the context of Yosemite has evolved over the years, its importance remains as an American archetype. Indeed, its significance grows. Even while exposed to new threats, Yosemite offers fresh promise to ours and future generations.

Evolution of a Park

At the same time it was created as a park, the Yosemite Grant was turned over to the State of California for administration. Congress later designated the lands surrounding the headwaters of the Tuolumne and Merced Rivers to become our third major national park in 1890, preceded only by Yellowstone and Sequoia. Criticized for mismanagement, the state returned Yosemite Valley and the Mariposa Grove to federal jurisdiction in 1906, creating the larger national park essentially as we know it today.

Rather than a failure, California's record of administration would have been exemplary, had officials followed the advice of Frederick Law Olmsted, America's greatest landscape architect. For a time, he chaired the Yosemite Commission, charged by the state to manage the Valley. With the clarity of wisdom that marked his other projects including Central Park in New York City, Olmsted prepared a plan. "The first thought to be kept in mind," he wrote, "is the preservation and maintenance as exactly as is possible of the natural scenery." He warned against any construction that would "unnecessarily obscure, distort, or detract from the dignity of the scenery." An unwilling state administration suppressed the plan, and it was ignored until rediscovered by Olmsted's biographer in 1952.

"Olmsted's work should be the master plan for the Valley," said Donald Fox, the park's landscape architect. "His thinking is as valid today as it was in 1865."

If that is the case, how did we end up with what we have? Rather than follow Olmsted's advice, managers of the Valley (both before and after its return to federal control) embarked on a 100-year binge of development. Automobiles, banned at first, were allowed to enter the park, and the Model T's soon lined up in Yosemite's first traffic jams. A commercial complex was built on the flood plain of the Merced River, and accommodations grew from the rustic few to the many—both rustic and luxurious. People drove at will through the meadows and camped wherever they found a vacant swatch of grass, tent cities being the cumulative effect.

Yosemite has always had its friends—people loving the place enough to take care of it—and so improvements were made that lessened the human impact on the Valley's soil. Most of the changes, coincidentally, allowed for the accommodation of more people. The roads, for example, were paved. Camping was restricted to established campgrounds so that the meadows could heal, but then the campgrounds grew in size to more than 2,000 sites. The flood-prone village was relocated to another site, converted from 22 buildings in 1925 to a sprawling complex in the 1960s. The Park Service closed some roads in the upper end of the Valley to auto traffic (reserving them for shuttle busses only), but the traffic on other roads increased, and bike trails were paved along the meadows.

One million visitors came to Yosemite National Park in 1954. Two million came in 1967. Twenty years later, in 1987, three million came, and only five years after that, nearly four million people arrived in the seven-mile-long valley that averages about a half a mile in width from the base of one mountainside to that of the other.

While diligent efforts resulted in the cleanup of some of the eyesores in and environmental insults to the Valley (such as a fenced-in zoo and leaking underground fuel tanks), Yosemite as it nears the year 2000 must confront a future of frenzied visitation increases, with no end in sight.

Many people will say that Yosemite is still the finest place in the world. But an increasing number now believe that Yosemite *used* to be the finest place in the world, that three million people a year in a seven-square-mile valley is too many, that it's just another overcrowded scene in an overcrowded state in an overcrowded world.

What is the effect of all these people on this gem of nature? Much of the scenery is durable. The waterfalls still throw their snowmelt for all to see. Though the meadows continue to be drained

Seeing What We Do

by ditches and are therefore dominated by introduced Kentucky bluegrass, they look natural compared to their past uses as hay-fields, pigpens, and parking lots.

But significant acreage falls into what can only be called sacrifice areas. Thirty miles of roads attract more than a million vehicles a year and cover perhaps three million square feet of Yosemite Valley with pavement, not counting 5,000 parking spots, which require 200 square feet each as a rule-of-thumb standard. Busses are a superior alternative to the automobiles that threaten to gridlock the Valley roads on busy days, but those diesel busses can be heard from the top of Half Dome. The campgrounds are as trampled as a county fairground the morning after the fair; beneath the conifer canopy, absolutely nothing grows. The Yosemite Lodge complex, including its

When one looks beyond

parking lot for many hundreds of cars, sits squarely in the viewshed of a key Valley highlight—Yosemite Falls. People's attention in this choice area is directed more at checking into a motel than at checking out the view.

When trails in Valley meadows proliferated and became deeply rutted, the Park Service nailed down boardwalks. In place of shoe-worn furrows, a wooden structure, chemically treated against rot, now snakes in bends and straightaways where once the meadow reigned.

A Sierra Club leader for many years, Dr. Edgar Wayburn, wrote about the Valley during the park's centennial year of 1990: "The traffic on the valley roads is distinctly urban in character. Amenities offered—from film development to bar service to banking—are just like those at home. The pall of smoke rising from campfires, buildings, and automobiles on busy holidays and summer weekends is not so different from the smog around other urban developments."

On the one hundredth birthday of the park, San Francisco Chronicle architecture critic Allan Temko went as far as to say, "Today's anniversary is not an occasion for celebration, since the park has merely survived, but for rueful questioning of our failure to cherish Yosemite as a place where our souls may be renewed, instead of a careless playground and entertainment resort."

My time spent in a Yosemite campground—in the cool, quiet month of March—was characterized by my demands that neighbors quit carrying on at 12:30 a.m., by the persistent idling of one neighbor's engine, the industrial chugging of another's electric generator, and by barking dogs. Campfire smoke saturated what had been fresh mountain air. Military aircraft flew so low that I could not hear my partner speak from five feet away, though overhead flights are supposedly regulated.

Make no mistake about it, while visiting the Valley I saw thousands of people who love and appreciate Yosemite. This was obvious because they sat and soaked up the experience. They walked and biked. They stood in awe at Bridalveil, Yosemite, and Vernal Falls. They lay napping in the meadows, they listened to the lessons of the ranger-naturalists, and they strolled at sunset along the Merced River. A few even wandered the Valley at night, when the moon illuminated the falls in a blur of white, and the shadows of the rocks lay huge and black on damp ground. Many of the people enjoying Yosemite from the comfort of their rented rooms or from their campsites also valued the place and cherished time spent beneath the granite walls.

I also saw great numbers of people shopping at a dozen or more retail outlets that specialize in the commodification of nature. People chatted, drank, and smoked in various bars, dressed up for dinner, and attended conferences at Curry Village, Yosemite Lodge, and the Ahwahnee Hotel. People watched TV, played bridge, and swam at the pool.

Few people object to any of these activities in their own places. But the question is: Why come to Yosemite to do them? Why take up Yosemite space to do them? These are, after all, the

the boundaries of Yosemite, the vexations

superlative seven square miles from a national total of nearly four million, and everyone knows that it is not difficult to find suitable sites elsewhere for shopping, swimming and the like. Indeed, the retail malls, traffic congestion, and workaday meetings are what people ostensibly go to a national park to escape.

No matter what you do, whether it's eating a $30 meal, catching frisbees, or attending the annual convention of any group that can afford to host its members here, Yosemite provides a better backdrop for it. Who can fault a soul for wanting to be here, regardless of the agenda? But fundamental problems haunt the Yosemite-as-a-backdrop notion. One of these is that people can lose sight of Yosemite as a natural gift. The scenery can become an adjunct to the road, cafeteria, postcards, ice skating rink, and accommodations, whether they be the Ahwahnee Hotel or a tent cabin on a concrete slab. To some, the development becomes an integral part of the scenery. They may consider the view to be enhanced by the roads and facilities, looking so much better than they do in the suburban strip back home.

For many other people, the crowds, cars, and development are reasons to stay away. These people, ironically, are not the ones who value the place the least, but the ones who value it the most. They are the people who desire the real Yosemite, defined here simply as Yosemite the way God made it.

Hired by the National Park Service to survey public opinion, Professor James H. Gramann of Texas A&M University predictably reported that people interviewed in the park were content with the quality of their visits. But Gramann underscored the inherent fallacy in his study: people who are unhappy with what the park has become are not there to be questioned. As the degree of urbiculture increases, people who prefer the natural scene stay away. The phenomenon is known as displacement. Gramann reported, "The inexorable trend has been toward greater numbers of visitors and more intensive development," all the time attracting a visitor with "increased tolerance for increasing numbers." Of course these people are happy with Yosemite. If you take the finest place on earth, and even if you degrade it substantially, it is still more desirable for vacationers than Fresno, Los Angeles, San Francisco or Tokyo.

Facing a troublesome twist on this problem, National Park Service Chief Naturalist Leonard McKenzie said, "In our work, we try to enhance visitor understanding and appreciation of Yosemite and to provoke in people a sense of inspiration. It's difficult to do that with visitors who are not receptive to it, or who don't have the time. The Park Service has developed the Valley to accommodate visitor use, and the park now attracts people who are insulated from the natural world by an unnecessary comfort zone of development. Many people are reluctant to get too far from their cars. It's frustrating to see the superficial ways in which many people use the park and to be unable to influence their perceptions or behavior."

of the world are out there, poised to rush in

Ranger-naturalist Ginger Burley described the challenge somewhat more graphically. "The problem we have today is like that of conducting a service in a great cathedral while bus load after bus load of tourists constantly marches in and out." The more the experience is trivialized, the less receptive the visitor is to Yosemite's message of reverence for the natural world.

This grim cycle seems to have no end. The more people come, the more the accommodation, even if it's as subtle as boardwalks instead of trails. The appearance and character of the park change. That change results in even more people, more accommodation, and ever less appeal to those seeking a natural Yosemite. "At some point," McKenzie added, "I hope that the process can be reversed to reflect a better balance between resource preservation and visitor accommodation."

Sharing this view, Yosemite's research scientist, Jan Van Wagtendonk, said, "Frederick Law Olmsted was right. In a national park, the focus of the activity should be on the resource. Golf at Wawona and the chef's holidays at the Ahwahnee have nothing to do with the resource. Nothing."

At the heart of the matter lies the question: what should the national parks be? In 1960, foreseeing the population pressures of the decades to come, the great national park historian, John Ise, wrote, "What we shall apparently have, then, is a system of national parks which, at the main points of interest, will not offer much of primeval quiet and serenity to the lover of nature, but will be overrun with millions of people … it will be merely one aspect of the transformation wrought in America by various factors, including our population explosion and the ubiquitous automobile, which are turning our fair land into a madhouse."

Congress mandated that the Park Service both protect the parks and provide for people's enjoyment. Is Yosemite Park protected if an experience of luminous wonder is replaced by one of boisterous rafters floating through the formerly inspiring scene of the Merced River, or by heavy traffic ringing the Valley like a race course?

It was the view of a recent Park Superintendent that more people can be accommodated at Yosemite without resource damage. He said that resource damage was the only reason to limit the amount of use. Any other rationale, such as a qualitative judgement about people's experiences, was thought to be unjustifiable. He said that more can be done to reinforce the landscape against harm, to disperse people, and to ameliorate congestion.

Believing that Yosemite's effect on people is a legitimate basis for park planning, Dean Malley said, "The more you have to contend with lots of people, the less you can enjoy the Yosemite experience." Malley represented the Yosemite Coalition, a park advocacy group. He added, "This place is worth more than the fast-food way of serving the public. You can have almost unlimited numbers of people if you just pave enough of Yosemite, and then take measures to make sure people stay on the pavement. Is this what we want? I don't think so. Yosemite is not Central Park."

if they haven't already.

Furthermore, there is little agreement that resource damage isn't being done, even as park facilities may become neater and more efficient. Research scientist Van Wagtendonk said, "Obviously, where you have development, roads, and reinforced walkways, you don't have meadows and forests. To me, that's damage. The question is, how much are we willing to accept and still have a park be a park?"

People including Joan Reiss, a wilderness advocate, and Dean Malley argue that, regardless of resource damage or the lack of it, the type of experience that people have in Yosemite is important. They object to a Disneyland, even if it would pose no environmental threat to this one-and-only place. They believe that the appreciation of Yosemite is the best use. They do not argue this point with any claim of superior taste, but for the simple reason that Yosemite is available nowhere else on Earth.

While people wanting to avoid the crowds in Yosemite Valley can steer clear of the cabin clusters and tourist emporia, their search for silence is futile. Any yen for solitude is rewarded only when hiding behind a rock, and even that grows more difficult to do as the "dispersal" plans become more effective and as the concessionaire aggressively markets Yosemite for the off-seasons, which scarcely exist anymore.

Many improvement efforts have aimed at making Yosemite Valley a less cluttered, more workable place. These measures include roped-off areas for oaks to regerminate, and traffic control. While they accomplish important purposes, they also accommodate additional people.

Looking more to the source of the problems, two viable means have been suggested to return Yosemite to a less crowded and quieter place, more conducive to what author and park analyst Joseph Sax called the "contemplative" experience, which he effectively argued is the best use of the national parks. One approach is simply to limit the number of people who are allowed to enter, much as the capacity of a concert hall or baseball stadium is set. Once the seats are sold, people are not given tickets to stand in the way of others.

The second approach is to design the park's infrastructure so that it doesn't appeal so much to people lacking interest in the natural Yosemite. A de-emphasis on shopping, conferences, dining, drinking, and the private automobile, which some people drive around and around Yosemite Valley, could all be examples of this approach. While denying access to no one, the resulting park would appeal less to people who prefer the increasingly urban aspect of developed Yosemite. Either approach requires planning, and good planning was once taken more seriously in Yosemite.

Triumph, Failure, and Persistence in Planning

A Yosemite planning effort was undertaken in the 1970s and became a model of public involvement in the National Park System. An unprecedented 60,000 people participated in the process that resulted in adoption of the General Management Plan of 1980.

In this landmark document, the Park Service stated, "The foremost responsibility of the National Park Service is to perpetuate the natural splendor of Yosemite ... The intent of the National Park Service is to remove all automobiles from Yosemite Valley and Mariposa Grove and to redirect development to the periphery of the park and beyond. Similarly, the essence of wilderness, which so strongly complements the Valley, will be preserved. The result will be that visitors can step into Yosemite and find nature uncluttered by piecemeal stumbling blocks of commercialism, machines, and fragments of suburbia ... "

Five goals were listed: to reclaim priceless natural beauty, to markedly reduce traffic congestion, to allow natural processes to prevail, to reduce crowding and to promote visitor understanding and enjoyment. The plan recommended that hundreds of structures be removed, and stated, "Once this development is gone from the park's most magnificent settings, the scenery that inspired the philosophy of John Muir ... will begin to be restored."

This new Bible for Yosemite was widely heralded as a turning point, a signal that the Valley would become a more natural place, more suitable for the appreciation of its intrinsic qualities. The Park Service officially adopted the plan just before the Reagan administration took office.

Few provisions of the plan were put into effect in the following decade. Traffic increased, and visitation grew dramatically. Only a few facilities were moved outside the Valley, some new ones were built, and nearly every structure that had been vacated was re-inhabited for some other function. No new roads were closed. Use of cars was not restricted. Many critics expressed concern that during the ten years following the plan's adoption, very little had been accomplished.

In a 1989 "General Management Plan Examination Report," Park Service officials stated that, in fact, many of the plan's goals had not been met. Rather than focus on ways to better meet the established goals, the report indicated that many of the plan's recommendations were not likely to be pursued in the near future. Instead, the report identified "potential changes," called for new "projections," and prescribed an "ongoing re-evaluation of essential services." In contrast to the plan, these conclusions were drawn without any public involvement and without participation from many critical Park Service officials in Yosemite—professionals who later reaffirmed their commitment to the original plan.

While a lack of funding can explain some of this imperfect progress, several million dollars were spent by the government to refurbish the rambling Wawona Hotel, for which the government received lease fees of $1,200 a year from the private concessionaire. About $76 million was spent on park infrastructure—water lines, sewer systems and the like. All of this may have been needed, but all of it further accommodated the tourist trade rather than reduced traffic, crowds and development, which were the forerunning goals of the plan.

"The solutions promoted by the General Management Plan *are* achievable, given the requisite will on the part of the National Park Service," said Bob Binnewies, who served as Yosemite superintendent when the plan was adopted. Pointing out the extensive public involvement that led to the plan, he added, "The real issue is what the plan stands for—the concern and expectations of the public."

So why was so little accomplished to make Yosemite a more natural, less congested place? History provides some of the answers. The National Park Service has always lacked vocal constituents, and the agency thereby promoted more use of the parks in order to generate support. With nearly eighty years of momentum, the trend continues, though a strong constituency now exists to protect the parks rather than to simply increase visitation.

Another factor is that elected officials are lobbied vigorously by retailers and developers from surrounding communities, people who equate more use, more traffic, and more development (both inside and outside the park) with livelihood and progress. Ironically, economic interests in "gateway" communities would benefit if development were moved out of the park and if cars were limited inside the park.

Some park officials blame the failure to improve Yosemite on a "lack of vision" owing to world views of individuals who climb the ranks within the agency, along with a very human propensity to "react" to problems rather than deal with their nettlesome sources. Fearing reprisal and criticism, top administrators demand that corrective actions be taken only when unquestionable resource damage can be shown. This passes the burden of proof to the scientific researchers, whose programs are poorly funded relative to the budgets for accommodating people's use of the park.

Perhaps more to the point, the private concessionaire lobbies for its interests. In 1989 the concessionaire sent more than 90,000 letters to former patrons urging them to write to the Park Service and demand more motel rooms and more parking spaces.

The result is that development in Yosemite Valley has not noticeably decreased and that the visitor population has grown phenomenally. There's an established ceiling of about 18,000 people at a time allowed in the seven-mile-long valley, and the Park Service superintendent stated that he saw little problem if crowds of that magnitude occurred on a daily basis.

Threats from Beyond

While the political boundaries of Yosemite are neat and ordered, the ecosystem boundaries are not. They run down the Merced and Tuolumne canyons and into the foothills of dazzling wildflowers in springtime, slopes as steep and green as in the Alps, turning golden-brown in summer. Onward through the chaparral belt of shrubs and dwarf oaks, the river canyons play host to deer herds that migrate from Yosemite for critical winter range. Mountain lions follow, depending on the deer for food. Bears migrate up and down, needing the habitat of both high and low country. The Sierra crest offers habitat to rare bighorn sheep that scramble down the eastern slope to their winter range in Toiyabe National Forest and on private land. And there, on the east side, Sierra snows melt into the biological wonder of Mono Lake, home to a spectacle of migrating birds.

When one looks beyond the boundaries of Yosemite—and you need not go far—threats to Yosemite's larger ecosystem are apparent everywhere. Near the southwest boundary, dams on the Merced River and its South Fork were proposed for power generation, but were defeated by citizen action in 1987. A similar dam on the Tuolumne River was halted in 1984; yet another was proposed in the 1990s for the Clavey River, just west of the park. The Los Angeles Department of Water and Power depleted Mono Lake of its flows, and for nearly twenty years, the Mono Lake Committee has sought to restore biological vitality to that unique body of water.

Logging proceeded apace in the national forests surrounding Yosemite, including the rich timber zone of middle Sierran elevations just to the west. Great gray owls of the park depend on national forest land as well as on private ranch land that has not been developed.

With some of the highest growth rates in the state, the foothill counties are being subdivided and built upon with little regard for local features or the greater ecosystem that extends into Yosemite. New homes and shopping centers result in bulldozed habitat, dried up streams and springs, and legions of house cats and dogs preying, with devastating effect, on birds and wildlife.

Over objections of the Park Service, irrigation districts in the Central Valley seeded Yosemite's clouds with silver iodide, failing to cause rain but dumping foreign chemicals on the park in an air-drop of industrial proportions.

Federal agencies have succeeded on some important points of ecosystem protection, such as designation of the Merced and Tuolumne Rivers, from their headwaters down through the foothills, as "National Wild and Scenic Rivers." Agencies have cooperated to develop prescribed fire management plans calling for prescribed burns that will, in effect, take the place of the frequent natural fires that commonly burned in the Sierra before suppression programs of the government existed. The prescribed burns are essential if disastrous fires—resulting from an unnatural build up of dead wood and flammable understory—are to be avoided.

Seeing the need for more cohesive protection, Sierra Club spokespersons have proposed an expanded national park, with boundaries extended southward to Kings Canyon National Park. To gain greater protection of public land in the critical lower-elevation areas adjacent to Yosemite, research scientist Jan Van Wagtendonk advocates a national recreation area where protection of the ecosystem would be stressed. Though some local communities oppose those ideas, Yosemite, Kings Canyon, and Sequoia National Parks generate $322 million a year in business revenue and sustain 7,000 jobs in Fresno County alone—benefits that could be jeopardized if the parks fail to sustain living ecosystems.

Even more insidious than habitat loss, air pollution from the Central Valley and the San Francisco Bay area causes ozone damage to one-third of the ponderosa and Jeffrey pine trees in

Yosemite—an ominous problem that continues to worsen. Amphibians in the park decline precipitously toward extinction, perhaps due to contaminated rainfall.

The problem of this presumably transparent medium of air is distressingly visible. The view westward from the peaks of Yosemite shows a sea of yellow-gray haze blanketing low elevations in the Central Valley each morning. The pall creeps eastward as daytime breezes rise over the mountains, until the haze infiltrates Yosemite Valley and wafts up to the Sierra crest, where the "Range of Light" has also become the range of acid rain. Ozone levels in the mountains often exceed those of Sacramento. The pollution is even worse in Sequoia and Kings Canyon National Parks, and worse yet in the national forest land of the San Bernardino Mountains, where trees have died on a massive scale. Is this the future of Yosemite?

While government-imposed controls have resulted in per-car decreases of air-borne pollutants in California, the growth rate of the state continued, negating many of the hard-earned and expensive air quality improvements. Yosemite Park Superintendent Michael Finley said, "A major problem of this park and others is the assault by air pollution. The long-term vision of Yosemite is bleak unless we do something about ozone and acid rain in the surrounding environment."

The contaminated air caused by Californians' ever-increasing dependence on the private automobile threatens the vitality of Yosemite, not to mention that of the rest of the Sierra Nevada, agricultural production in the Central Valley, and the health of people in all the state's urban areas. The air quality problem saliently illustrates that no place is an island in the modern world of fossil fuel dependence and increasing energy consumption.

At the source of many of Yosemite's problems is the rate of population growth in California. The state has been growing by 700,000 people annually—more than the population of San Francisco. Virtually all state residents live within a one-day drive of Yosemite. Thus, the greater Yosemite ecosystem of social forces in 1993 included 32 million Californians plus their 25 million automobiles (a fleet growing by 300,000 a year).

The Park as a Model

While the responsibility lies with all Californians for restoring the health of their state and reviving the dream of a promising and liveable homeland, the fate of Yosemite is of special concern to people here and throughout the nation. Many overriding threats to Yosemite originate beyond the park's borders. Some people argue that little can be done in Yosemite to influence those threats; however, an unprecedented opportunity exists within this celebrated national park.

California, the nation, and the world need a vision of a better place and a better way of sustaining that place. What finer example than Yosemite? Long regarded as the ultimate scenic landscape in America and as a center of reverence for the natural world, what better site exists to institute the principles of sustainability and environmental restoration?

Air pollution from California's Central Valley and coast threatens the ecological integrity of the park; private automobiles in cities and suburbs are the principal source of the pollution. What more appropriate signal of environmental reform could be given than to reduce sharply the number of cars in Yosemite Valley? The advantages of protecting the Valley in this way are lucidly spelled out in the General Management Plan. The direct reduction of pollution could be substantial, especially if effected by people's use of public transit originating in their home towns.

But that is not the main point. The main point here is that the park can become a model of reform and a guidepost for cutting our dependence on polluting cars—proof that, in fact, our society can change in response to real needs.

Indeed, how can the National Park Service, Yosemite enthusiasts and others who are concerned about the death of pine forests and loss of species owing to air pollution expect the state of California and its residents to solve a problem as ingrained as driving to and from work and shopping malls, if Yosemite itself cannot cut dependence on cars in such an isolated and controlled environment as a national park? The reason for failing to curb auto use here differs little from the reason for failing to curtail upwind air pollution that migrates so destructively into the park. That reason is the unwillingness to relinquish even slightly the privilege of driving cars wherever and whenever we want. But if Yosemite can't reduce auto dependence, how can California do it?

Plans to minimize the numbers of cars in Yosemite have been drawn up by the government and by non-profit groups concerned about the park. The General Management Plan of 1980 stated, "Increasing automobile traffic is the single greatest threat to enjoyment of the natural and scenic qualities of Yosemite. In the near future, automobile congestion will be greatly reduced by restricting people's use of their cars and increasing public transportation."

A cutback in cars would not force people to walk or bicycle in, though doing so from the edges of the Valley may become a more rewarding experience without the plague of traffic on both sides of the Merced River. Reductions in cars can be accomplished by instituting economic incentives to leave vehicles behind, by establishing parking areas at the fringe of Yosemite with bus service into the Valley, and by restricting people's continuing use of cars if they do drive into the Valley. Some of these approaches, such as the last one, would cost little, and some would require a relatively large investment, but a complex of three parking areas at the park's periphery with connecting busses would have totalled far less than the recent improvements to the water and sewer system in the Valley.

If Yosemite can be a model of transportation reform, then it can also be a model for coping with population growth. A statewide increase of 6 million people per decade taxes not only California's environment and living space but also the entire skein of government and social systems, from water supply and roads to schools and welfare. Many people now agree that unlimited population growth is not to anyone's advantage. In fact, runaway growth is the cause of the demise of so much that has been valued in California—open space, clean air and water, liveable communities, and friendly neighborhoods (not to mention a balanced budget for state government). Various measures that involve solutions can be taken. These may be centered around family planning, public information, and economic incentives for slower growth. Yet, public officials refuse to grapple with the controversial issue.

The burden of too many people is tragic enough in stressed-out cities and beleaguered landscapes across the state, but for Yosemite National Park to be paralyzed by the same reluctance to address the question of popu-

lation growth threatens the park and the very essence of the Yosemite experience. What will remain of this wonderland and of the extraordinary contribution it can offer to people when visitation reaches 6 million, 8 million, or 10 million?

It should be noted here that the park's plan does limit the number of visitors to Yosemite Valley to about 18,000 at any one time. The daily total, however, can be considerably more. The ceiling is based on parking spaces. Few people participating in the plan envisioned that the prescribed maximum visitation would occur on a regular basis. Rather, it was regarded as the level bordering total malfunction that might be tolerated for a few days a year, if absolutely necessary. Yet, nothing now prevents those levels from being reached all the time.

Research scientist Jan Van Wagtendonk pointed out, "In many places in the world, the numbers of people are successfully kept to reasonable levels. We do that at Denali and elsewhere in the National Park System. Why not Yosemite?"

Chief Naturalist Leonard McKenzie said, "Until we set and implement use limits with priority on resource protection rather than accommodating people, we will continue to see degradation of the park."

Much is made of Yosemite's role as a symbol of nature in America late in the nineteenth century and of the early success in preserving this natural wonder. Congratulations for past accomplishments are fine, but perhaps it is time to look at the present, and at the future. Now, a century after our first successes in protecting this park, Yosemite can again become a symbol of national progress. Here we can recognize that everything in the natural world is limited, including the acreage of Yosemite Valley and its ability to accommodate people. Decisions here could show that it is better to limit growth than to irrevocably lose the qualities of the place that attracted people in the first place.

California, the nation, and the world need a vision of a better place and a better way of sustaining that place.

Much as actions a hundred years ago set wise precedents for protection in the National Park System, today's actions could be felt as ripples beyond this valley. How we as a people care for Yosemite will give a strong indication of how we will care for the Earth generally in the coming decades.

The alternative to taking effective action is pure tragedy—a Yosemite of trivialized outdoor experience, a sacred valley where people come to see nature but find only the frenzy that unlimited growth brings to all overcrowded places.

An American Symbol

Here, where the national park idea was born in 1864, we are left with the wise guidance of Frederick Law Olmsted, the exuberant determination of John Muir, the heritage of a great national park, and the challenge of sustaining that greatness amid intense pressures of conflict and population growth. But most of all, we are left with Yosemite itself. The rock-bound landscape endures. As park historian Jim Snyder said, "Sometimes when we look up at the walls of granite we say, 'Thank God. At least that can't be hurt.' "

Working since 1931 as the park's beloved naturalist, Carl Sharsmith emphasized his message of humbleness and care for this land: "We should feel grateful that we're a part of the picture." Perhaps more than anything, the old ranger's advice captures the appropriate role of people in Yosemite: feeling grateful.

Forever a landmark, Yosemite remains a symbol of what is best about America—a place of biological breadth and wonder, an enclave of inspiring beauty, and a refuge where future generations can see the finest of our inheritance. It remains, for now, a place with all the power to open people's eyes and minds to the glory of the universe, to the feelings of love and stewardship that must abide within us if we are to have a successful journey through the coming decades on planet Earth. The challenge remains to treat this land with the respect it deserves. Only then will we have kept the promise of preservation and realized the promise of wildness.

Portfolio
Two

previous page
Yellow Aspens

Lee Vining Canyon

Clouds at sunset over Kuna Crest from

Tioga Tarns

Pine sapling growing out of crack
in glacially carved granite

Glen Aulin

Redbud along the Merced River

Merced River Canyon

Autumn color

Merced River

Giant sequoia trees

Mariposa Grove

Forest scene

Happy Isles

Maples and boulders

Yosemite Valley

Sunset reflections, spring thaw

Tenaya Lake

previous page left
Lupine

Wawona

previous page right
Corn Lilies

Summit Meadows

Glacial polish at sunset

Glen Aulin

Aspen and sage
in autumn, late afternoon light

Silver Lake, Inyo National Forest

Black oak and El Capitan

Yosemite Valley

Jeffrey pine silhouetted at sunset

Sentinel Dome

Horsetail Fall

El Capitan

Black oaks in fog at sunset

El Capitan Meadow

Winter storm

Three Brothers

Black oaks

**Merced River and
El Capitan**

Spring storm

Yosemite Valley

Alder and granite boulder

Yosemite Valley

Ice and grass

Yosemite Valley

Black oak branches in winter

Yosemite Valley

Blue ice detail

Yosemite Valley

Ice pattern on the
Tuolumne River

Tuolumne Meadows

Horsetail ferns
in snow

El Capitan Meadow

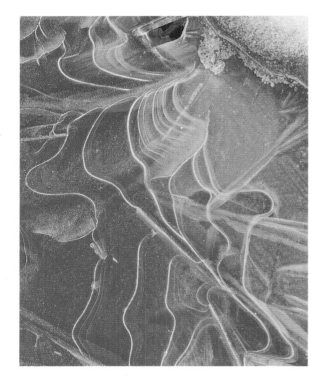

Winter sunset

El Capitan

Half Dome and elm tree, winter

Cook's Meadow

There is little doubt about Yosemite's uniqueness and importance in the world. It has significance for humankind, as well as for the individual. Yosemite has had a profound effect on my own life. This is a place where I have found peace and beauty. Here I have often been reminded of my con-

Observations of the Photographer

nection with all living things. I have watched the light make its play in endless variations on this landscape, reveled in Yosemite's grand scene, and meditated on its intimate details.

I first arrived in Yosemite in 1962 when I was eight. My only recollections of that visit are of the spectacular "fire falls" and an exciting ride on the old Tioga Road. I am certain, however, that my fate was strongly affected by that early journey.

I began photographing in the summer of 1973 in Glacier National Park, where I was working during summer break from college. My "equipment" consisted of a Kodak Instamatic camera. I wanted to record my adventures backpacking through the park, and share them with family and friends. I soon graduated to a 35 millimeter camera—an old Pentax Spotmatic. With this camera and the addition of a tripod, I began to make a few images that showed promise, and, more importantly, reflected my experiences.

When I graduated from the University of Colorado in 1976 with a degree in Environmental Conservation, I knew a career in resource management was not for me. Inspired by the powerful photographs of great artists such as Minor White, Wynn Bullock, Edward Weston, Ansel Adams, Ernst Haas and Eliot Porter, I chose photography. I wanted to pursue a life that combined wild places and art.

In 1977, I received a call from the National Park Service in Yosemite offering me a maintenance job at White Wolf in Yosemite's high country. With images of the park dancing in my head, I accepted the position and moved to the park. A few years later, I landed a job as the photographer at The Ansel Adams Gallery. My career was launched. I have been living in the park ever since.

Although I feel that I now know Yosemite intimately, I have by no means explored the park thoroughly. While these images represent limited ramblings, they do reflect the places that draw me back again and again. Different people, when experiencing the park, have different places where they feel the most comfortable, where they feel energized and at peace. It may be beside a alpine lake, in the spray of a waterfall, on top of a peak or lying in a meadow in the sun. These special places rejuvenate us, and in my case, stimulate some of my best work.

Photography is a quiet, contemplative activity of me. It is a time to experience my environment fully. Yosemite has many private spots where I can explore undisturbed. As I explore, I approach my subject gently. I am inspired by Minor White, the Zen-influenced photographer, who wrote, "Be still with yourself, until the object of your attention affirms your presence." One needs time, be it hours or weeks or years, to absorb one's surroundings, to learn a place's moods, light and weather. I am not compelled to make a photograph every time I wander about. When I find a scene that moves me, it is irresistible. I am commanded by the light and the subject to arrange a composition in the ground glass. Ansel Adams said that a great photograph is the artistic equivalent of the emotions of the photographer at the moment of exposure. When the emotion of the experience is strong, then so can be the image.

The photographs I enjoy making most are those that rely on my perception rather than the spectacle of the scene. I prefer to isolate details of a scene, often to the point of abstraction. I have tried to learn the art of seeing, then revealing, the essence of my subject. When the composition is simplified, its essence can come through. When the content or orientation of a photograph is not obvious, the artist can call forth an enigmatic feeling in the viewer.

I would rather make an image that poses a question, not one with answers. A photograph should intrigue and arouse curiosity in the viewer. I appreciate images that grow on me and endure. Many works have initial impact, but explain themselves immediately, then quickly fade from memory. To avoid the cliché is a considerable challenge in Yosemite because so many images have been published, and because people now have preconceived notions about how Yosemite should appear. With patience and a spirit of exploration, unique photographs can still be made.

This book contains my personal view of Yosemite. It is my hope that it will help you see the park in a new and refreshing light. Yosemite is still a place worth exploring in depth—far into the backcountry or a few hundred yards off the road. In both its grandeur and its intimate landscapes, beauty abounds here. Offering renewal and rejuvenation, it is still full of magic and mystery. This is the Yosemite worth preserving. May the spirit of Yosemite endure.

WILLIAM NEILL
Yosemite, 1994

The photographs within this book were made primarily with a Wista 4 x 5 metal field camera. Lenses of 90, 150, 210, and 360 millimeter focal lengths were used. A variety of film was employed—Kodak Ektachrome 64, Polaroid ProChrome 100, and Fujichrome Velvia are all represented here. Two images were made using Nikon 35mm equipment, and exposed on Fujichrome and Kodak Kodachrome films. Limited edition prints are made on Ilfochrome Classic (formerly Cibachrome) material which gives rich colors and fine detail. A process known as contrast-masking is used to enhance the prints and better reflect the artist's interpretation of the scene.

Notes on the Photographs

PAGES 2–3

Black oak branches in winter, Yosemite Valley, 1994
Following an intense morning of shooting the aftermath of a February storm, I headed towards home feeling tired and satisfied. It was mid-morning, and though the light seemed to be poor for more photography, I stopped at my favorite meadow to linger. As I talked to another photographer, a mass of clouds blocked the sun and softened the harshness of the scene. Back to the van for my camera and more film! These dark branches were starkly outlined against the fresh white snow. Because the depth of field was considerable, I used a small aperture to define the detail and flatten the perspective.

PAGES 4–5

Black oaks leafing out in spring,
Yosemite Valley, 1986
See notes for page 22.

PAGES 6–7

Half Dome viewed from spring snow field on
Sentinel Dome, 1991
The view from Sentinel Dome is a 360° panorama that includes Half Dome, the Clark Range, Tenaya Canyon, Cathedral Peak and Mount Conness. For many visitors, it is the best place to gain a perspective of the park's size. I have always found it an uplifting perspective with its reminder that most of the park is wilderness.

PAGE 8

Yosemite Valley shrouded in mist, 1994
On the morning after a heavy spring rain, low clouds were sifting through the trees on the Valley floor. The sun backlit the fog for a strikingly graphic effect. I used a telephoto lens to zero in on just the trees and mist, and the panoramic format accentuated the sweep of the forest across the Valley.

PAGE 10

Sunset from the summit of
Mount Hoffmann, 1986
Alone, I hiked up the peak in the late afternoon. I had the mountain to myself as the sun eased down in the west. The colors were amplified by the smoke of a September forest fire. I photographed quickly, trying various compositions. Finally finished, I sat down to enjoy the silence and the view before returning to the trailhead by flashlight. Mount Hoffmann is the geographical center of the park. The angle of view of this photograph is north into a wilderness that few people ever see.

PAGE 12

El Capitan and Merced River, winter sunset,
Gates of the Valley, 1984
The Gates of the Valley vista brings together the classic elements of the Merced River, El Capitan, Cathedral Rocks and Bridalveil Fall in a quintessential Yosemite view. In the winter, fog often rises off the river here. On this evening, lingering clouds on the face of El Capitan turned orange at sunset and were reflected in the river. While this location is usually crowded at dusk, I worked alone and undisturbed as I created this image.

PAGE 14

Autumn leaves, Fern Spring, Yosemite Valley, 1984
An autumn storm had just passed through the Sierra, covering the ground with colorful leaves. Fern Spring was shaded, but it reflected a clear blue sky in its waters. I was pleased by the way the cool-colored highlights contrasted with the fall tones of the leaves.

PAGE 19

Bistort blooming in Crane Flat Meadows, 1986
The meadows of the park's high country are favorite summer destinations of many Yosemite regulars. Even Crane Flat, a large meadow complex on the Tioga Road, has many hidden and secluded spots to explore. On a walk one summer evening, I found this particularly dense patch of bistort. Good photography is a highly selective process—one must seek out the best light, the trees with the most dynamic graphic lines, or flowers that are the thickest and lushest. The perfect location or composition is rarely reached randomly. The process involves multiple choices as one goes about finding the right combination of elements.

PAGES 20–21

Aspen reflections on the Tuolumne River,
Glen Aulin, 1993
When I hiked into Glen Aulin, the glassy but rapid Tuolumne River reflected an aspen grove on its far bank. Using a panoramic format, I was able to display the graphic qualities of the repeating white trunks across the long frame. This grove, isolated from the trail by the tumultuous river, has likely seen few people over the centuries.

PAGE 22

Black oaks leafing out in spring,
Yosemite Valley, 1986
There are a few days each spring when the oak leaves begin to bud and take on an amazingly fresh hue of green. I caught these oaks at just the right time. The day was cloudy and provided the soft light I prefer.

PAGES 26–27

Clearing summer storm clouds, Gates of the Valley,
Yosemite Valley, 1985
By August in the Valley, the Merced River has receded. Thunderstorms roll through regularly on the hot afternoons. Both these seasonal conditions contributed to this image. Reflections in the still river were clear, and the bands of light coming through the clouds were spectacular.

PAGE 48

Yellow pines in snow, Yosemite Valley, 1990

The wet snow from this storm weighed on these pine trees. The wintry scene provided conditions for an almost monochromatic photograph. I am often attracted to subjects with a limited color palette.

PAGE 49

Floating ice and cliffs, Ellery Lake,
Inyo National Forest, California, 1993

I used a long lens to pull the cliffs forward, and the subtle side lighting across the cliffs gave this image its contrast of strength and softness. The passage of winter to spring is really a transition into summer at the high elevations. The alpine lakes often thaw within a few days.

PAGE 50

Glacial erratics, late afternoon light near
Olmsted Point, 1990

Deposited by ancient glaciers, these rocks cast long shadows on this granite floor. Signs of the earth's geological processes such as erosion, exfoliation and glaciation fascinate me, and I am astounded by the vast time that was involved in sculpting the land.

PAGE 51

Glacial erratic and clouds near Tenaya Lake, 1986

This rock is about fifteen feet high. Using my wide angle lens, I was able to include the whole rock while keeping the trees small in the background. I lined up the cumulus clouds so they seemed to emanate from the rock itself.

PAGES 52–53

Cedars and rock circle, Merced River, 1986

The high water level in park rivers and streams is usually reached between May and July. During the runoff, there are many places in the Valley where the Merced River floods. Walking along the river in June, I discovered these partly-submerged trees and rocks. Because the sun had dropped below the canyon wall, the light was low. A two minute exposure blurred the rapidly moving water as it reflected the twilight sky.

PAGE 55

Cloud reflections and grasses,
Tuolumne Meadows, 1983

This seemingly straightforward shot required between ten and fifteen minutes of lining up the clouds so that they reflected clearly in the pond. Because the clouds were moving, I had to work quickly to set the camera position, take a meter reading, place the film holder in the camera back, and expose the film before they moved out of position. It took considerable effort to transform an ordinary picture into something more.

PAGES 56–57

Dogwood tree blooming along the Merced River,
Yosemite Valley, 1989

I love to photograph the dogwoods when they start to bloom. A cloudy day gave me the soft light I prefer to work with, and the river was beginning to rise with snowmelt. The long exposure smoothed the water, which provided a simple background for the dogwood branches.

PAGE 57

Vernal Fall and maple tree at the base of
Vernal Fall, 1990

Unique perspectives for photography are rare in Yosemite, but individuals with a sense of exploration and some imagination can still find them. This photograph was taken from a difficult-to-attain location. The brilliant light coming through the leaves, casting shadows on the granite wall, compensated me for my efforts to reach it.

PAGES 58–59

Clouds and reflections, Cathedral Rocks,
Yosemite Valley, 1993

After several years of drought, the spring snowmelt once again filled this pond. I waded into the shallow water for a clearer view of the reflection and to avoid some potentially distracting foreground elements. The lovely morning clouds added nicely to the composition.

PAGE 60

Black oaks and Cathedral Rocks,
Yosemite Valley, 1984

For many years I drove by these trees on my way home from work. Only rarely in winter do the twilight and mist combine with them as in this photograph. I attempted the shot on several occasions, over several years, without success. After many attempts to find the right composition, my practice runs finally paid off. When the conditions were just right, I was able to make the image I had visualized. The photograph embodies for me Yosemite as temple and sanctuary.

PAGE 62

Cottonwoods and Merced River, autumn,
Yosemite Valley, 1980

The autumn colors in Yosemite are relatively muted by New England standards. Nonetheless, the mixture of brilliant light, fall foliage and towering cliffs is matchless here. These were the most brilliantly yellow cottonwoods I have seen in my years at the park. The river was nearly still and allowed these great reflections.

PAGES 68–69

Swimming pool, Yosemite Lodge, 1983

This photograph does not immediately suggest Yosemite, but its subject represents an element of the Yosemite environment. The pool is only a few hundred yards from splendid swimming holes in the Merced River.

PAGE 71

Visitors, Glacier Point, 1984

Glacier Point offers the visitor a spectacular view of Yosemite Valley, Half Dome and the high country. This image depicts a quiet afternoon as far as crowds go. The last time I stopped, there were nearly 100 people at this spot listening to a ranger talk. I was happy to see so many visitors learning about the park and enjoying the vista, but the crowded conditions spoiled the experience for me.

PAGE 73

Parking lot, Curry Village, 1993

The parking lot at Curry Village is normally packed with vehicles. Finding a place to park here presents the same challenges as parking in a major city.

PAGE 74

Clouds over Yosemite Valley from
Tunnel View, 1984

The morning clouds in this image served as a lens shade and enabled me to photograph into the sun without the problem of flare. The lighting and the haze accentuate the classic shapes of the cliffs.

PAGES 78–79

Yellow aspens, Lee Vining Canyon,
Inyo National Forest, California, 1983

Just east of Tioga Pass is Lee Vining Canyon. Full of aspens, willows and sage, it lies at the western edge of the Great Basin of Nevada, Utah and Oregon. The still air and quiet light of morning allowed me to make a sharp image with rich saturation. I simplified the color combination to yellow leaves and whitish branches.

PAGE 100

Black oaks, Merced River and El Capitan,
Yosemite Valley, 1985

My best winter photographs are made during or right after a snowstorm. Perhaps the freshness of the new fallen snow is what distinguishes these images. It was snowing lightly when this exposure was made. My first instinct was to put on a wide-angle lens and include all of El Capitan. The medium focal length lens I chose revealed the power of El Capitan's cliffs without describing the entire monolith.

PAGE 101

Spring storm, Yosemite Valley, 1986

After a night of heavy rain, I drove up early in the morning to Tunnel View. The clouds hanging over the Valley floor were illuminated from behind. This was one instance when luck worked in my favor. In a hundred other visits to this spot, I have not encountered such dramatic conditions.

PAGE 102

Ice and grass, Yosemite Valley, 1982

I made this image in early November when the nights had dropped below freezing but the grasses in the meadows had not turned brown. The white ice and green grasses formed a poetic design. By mid-day, the frozen tapestry had melted away.

PAGE 103

Alder and granite boulder, Yosemite Valley, 1984

The similarity of these tree trunks and the rock wall behind them caught my attention. I eliminated adjacent objects to heighten the camouflage effect of the subjects. I exposed the photograph to accentuate the detail and was pleased with the way the edge lighting on the trunk gave a glow to the image.

PAGES 104–105

Black oak branches in winter,
Yosemite Valley, 1994

This image was made at the same time as the photograph appearing on pages 2-3; a panoramic back was used for that image and this one was exposed to a full frame sheet of 4 x 5 film.

PAGE 106 (LEFT)

Ice pattern on the Tuolumne River,
Tuolumne Meadows, 1986

I moved in close to the ice to isolate the lines and curves. I spent much time working with the relationships of the lines of ice to the edge of the frame before I achieved the orientation shown here.

PAGE 106 (RIGHT)

Horsetail ferns in snow, El Capitan Meadow,
Yosemite Valley, 1984

Composing this image was a slow and deliberate process. Working in a large area, I walked back and forth for at least 15 minutes before I found a spot where the shapes worked together in my viewfinder. The exact positioning of the camera was difficult because the lines of the ferns would merge and overlap, and I wanted to maintain as much spacing between lines as possible. The even light of an overcast day helped flatten the perspective and accentuate the pattern.

PAGE 107

Blue ice detail, Yosemite Valley, 1982

I found this patch of ice at the edge of a small pond. The sky's deep blue color is reflected in the shaded ice.

PAGE 109

Winter sunset on El Capitan,
Yosemite Valley, 1992

I rarely photograph this classic view of El Capitan, but the fresh snow and clouds at sunset were hard to pass up. Transformed by exceptional light and weather, the scene was no longer ordinary. The good light was fading fast so I worked hastily. Over the years I have learned to work quite rapidly with my view camera when I need to.

PAGES 110–111

Half Dome and elm tree in winter, 1990

A January storm left several feet of snow in the Valley. As the clouds began to break up in late afternoon, a shaft of light struck the elm while Half Dome brooded in the background. By sunset, the sky was clear.

PAGE 112

Frosted grasses in Bridalveil Meadow, 1992

The heavy frost of the grasses gave this meadow a delicate tone and texture. I looked for a spot to photograph where the lines of the grasses moved interestingly through the frame and back to the boulder at the top of the image.

Acknowledgments

When I first moved to Yosemite in 1977, I hoped someday to publish a book of the photographs I created here. There are many people whose friendship, encouragement, support and inspiration have helped my dream materialize. I can't list each of them, but I want to thank all of you.

Ansel Adams, whose spirit still rambles the "Range of Light," set a standard of excellence for me, though our acquaintance was brief. He encouraged me to develop my own vision of Yosemite. Also, the staff of The Ansel Adams Gallery in Yosemite, past and present, has been a source of support and friendship.

I want to thank the Yosemite Association staff for its hard work, not only on this project but on many others that benefit the park. Steve Medley deserves special credit for this book. He saw my vision and refined it. His concern for the park, and for the concept and quality of the book, is reflected herein. Thanks, too, to Lucille Tenazas for her elegant design.

And finally, undying thanks to my kindred spirit, Sadhna.

WILLIAM NEILL

I would like to express my gratitude to Steven Medley of the Yosemite Association. It was he who conceived of the book and brought it to publication, offering me the freedom to write as I saw fit, while providing wise guidance whenever I needed it. Yosemite and the rest of the Sierra would do well if many more people had his dedication to these extraordinary places.

TIM PALMER